Surrey & Sussex

Edited By Megan Roberts

First published in Great Britain in 2019 by:

Young Writers
Remus House
Coltsfoot Drive
Peterborough
PE2 9BF
Telephone: 01733 890066
Website: www.youngwriters.co.uk

All Rights Reserved
Book Design by Ashley Janson
© Copyright Contributors 2019
SB ISBN 978-1-78988-417-3
Printed and bound in the UK by BookPrintingUK
Website: www.bookprintinguk.com
YB0401EZ

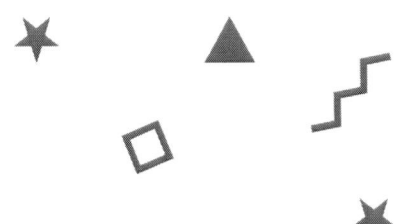

FOREWORD

Dear Reader,

Are you ready to get your thinking caps on to puzzle your way through this wonderful collection?

Young Writers are proud to introduce our new poetry competition, *My First Riddle*, designed to introduce Reception pupils to the delights of poetry. Riddles are a great way to introduce children to the use of poetic expression, including description, similes and expanded noun phrases, as well as encouraging them to 'think outside the box' by providing clues without giving the answer away immediately. Some pupils were given a series of riddle templates to choose from, giving them a framework within which to shape their ideas.

Their answers could be whatever or whoever their imaginations desired; from people to places, animals to objects, food to seasons. All of us here at Young Writers believe in the importance of inspiring young children to produce creative writing, including poetry, and we feel that seeing their own riddles in print will ignite that spark of creativity.

We hope you enjoy riddling your way through this book as much as we enjoyed reading all the entries.

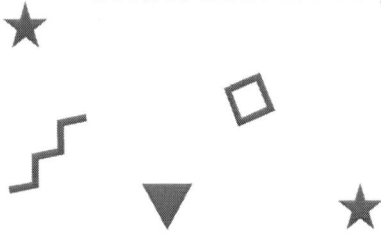

CONTENTS

Arundel CE Primary School, Arundel

May Sonsthagen (4)	1
Tahlia Aston (4)	2
Ella Slade (4)	3
Zayn Keane (4)	4
Tyreece Ford (5)	5
Max Withall (5)	6
Douglas Pacey (5)	7
Riley Hummerstone (4)	8

Audley Primary School, Caterham

Oscar Eacott-May (4)	9
Maia Quarmby (5)	10
Tommy Pendino (5)	11
Eli Pocock (5)	12
Henry Downs (5)	13
Hannah Scourfield (5)	14
Harrison Bennett (4)	15
Zayn Uddin (4)	16
Ethan Sherriff (5)	17
Jake Quarmby (5)	18
Charlie Lewis Mons (5)	19
Jack Gittins (4)	20
Lois Elsley (5)	21
Cohen Wright (4)	22
Isla Reynolds (4)	23
Sebastian Mansfield (4)	24
Emilia Bontas (5)	25
Amy May Beck (4)	26
Robbie Seal (5)	27
Sophia Myrmus (5)	28
Zion Edwards (4)	29
Charlie Cox (4)	30

Eryn Llewellyn Bayliss (4)	31
Michael Deiana (5)	32
Pearse Lewis (5)	33
Sienna Smith (5)	34
Beatrice Ramsey (4)	35
Phoebe Hayman (4)	36
Louie Gillespie (4)	37
Morganna Evans (4)	38

Brighton College Nursery, Pre-Prep And Prep School, Brighton

Jasmine Sandhu (5)	39
Aryav Clitus (5)	40
Laurence Fox (5)	41
Amaury David Rowe-Roberts (5)	42
Elizabeth Rosa Oliveri (4)	43
Ariana Keely (4)	44
Alexander Putra Downes-Yusuf (5)	45
Zak Helalat (4)	46
Maia Warren-Lewis (4)	47
Eden Warren-Lewis (4)	48
Jaclyn Yap (4)	49
Jake Munslow (5)	50
Shu Yuan Wang (5)	51
Ellon Xu (5)	52
Arjun Balakrishnan Banani (4)	53
Annabel Elizabeth Downes-Yusuf (5)	54
Aiden Chowdhury (4)	55
Eden Raiss (4)	56
Zach Field (4)	57

Broadwater CE Primary School, Worthing

Aoife Cassell (5)	58
Wilfred Oscar Miles (4)	59
Sophie Hollisey-McLean (5)	60
Ella Roberts (4)	61
Ava van der Mark (4)	62
Ellis Tricker (5)	63
Olivia Jenner McWilton (5)	64
Ava Sparkes (4)	65
Lucas Peckham (4)	66
Ethan Welikele (5)	67
Darwyn Raine Buller (5)	68
Alice Monk (4)	69
Elliot Samuel Smith (4)	70
Bebe Stratten (5)	71
Otto George-Holgate (5)	72
Stanley Robert Spencer (5)	73
Seth Martin (5)	74
Stanley Laycock (4)	75
Liam Condon (5)	76
Thomas Rogers (4)	77
Judith Emerson (5)	78
Ella Kinnear (4)	79
Tim Le Tian Yu (5)	80
Dereks Lazdans (5)	81
Dylan Thompson (4)	82
Layla Crystal Gadsby-Pullen (5)	83
Noah Wetherill (4)	84
Marco Li (6)	85
Reuben Thomas (4)	86
Joel Powell-Staggs (4)	87
Samuel Croft (4)	88
Raife Bird (4)	89
Jack Spicer (4)	90
Seb Sparkes (4)	91
Charlie Scrase (4)	92
Hendrix Batchelor-Kent (4)	93
Lottie Olivia Bell (4)	94
Jaxson Hughes (4)	95

Chyngton Primary School, Seaford

Mia Pearson (4)	96

Essendene Lodge School, Caterham

Harry Whittington (4)	97
Sadie Vernon (4)	98
Calum Grippman (5)	99
Harvey Vigor-Messenger (5)	100
Teddy Scarffe (4)	101
Isabella Ndumiyana (5)	102

Kew Riverside Primary School, Richmond

Eveleigh Sutton (5)	103
Vasco Ramos (5)	104

Krishna Avanti Primary School, Croydon

Yuv Desai (5)	105
Eva Desai (5)	106
Vihaan Ravani (4)	107

Northiam Primary School, Northiam

Ethan Penfold (4)	108
Florence Sansom (4)	109
Olly Jones (5)	110
Marnie Buss (5)	111

Notre Dame Preparatory School, Cobham

Mariam El Mayet (5)	112
Anika Karandikar (5)	113
Agata Muzinska (5)	114

Reedham Park School, Purley

Lucy Jansen (4)	115
Max Stock (5)	116
Aprayer Grant (5)	117
Blake Joubert (5)	118
Zara Yasamine Anwar (4)	119

Send CE Primary School, Send

Isla Ross (4)	120
Fearne Jones (4)	121
Archie Leigh Darren Chantry (5)	122
Benjamin Warne (5)	123
Olivia Lunnon (4)	124
Joshua Patrick Lunt (5)	125
Florence Booth (5)	126
Ada Reuben (4)	127
Mali Reuben (4)	128
Eve Ellis (5)	129
Teddy Blackwell (5)	130
Sophia Jessica Penny (5)	131
Rosie Walles (5)	132
Isla Wilson (5)	133
Alana Jean Kelly (5)	134
Jackson James Adams (5)	135
Phoebe Gayle Maritz (5)	136
Alexander Herwig (4)	137
Gracie Del La Rue (4)	138
Isla D'Auria (4)	139

Shrewsbury House Pre-Preparatory School, Esher

Theo Gibbard (4)	140
Taran Singh Tulsi (5)	141
Zakaria Rafiq (4)	142
Harley Joseph Sykes (4)	143
Ted William Kennedy (5)	144
Oliver McIlroy (4)	145
Charlie Hebburn (4)	146
George Olivier (4)	147
Senan Lousse (4)	148
Benjamin Higginson (4)	149
Isaac Boamah (4)	150
Ibrahim Rafiq (4)	151

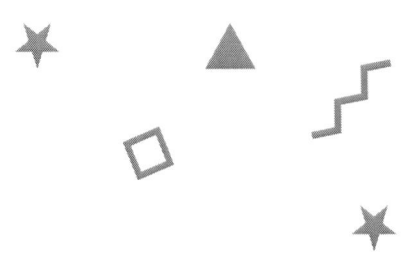

THE RIDDLES

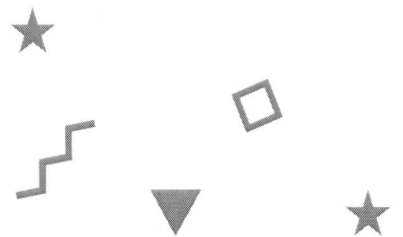

May's First Riddle

What could it be?
Follow the clues and see.

It looks like **a horse**.
It sounds like *clip, clop*.
It smells like **fluff**.
It feels like **a flower cushion**.
It tastes like **a flower**.

Have you guessed what it could be?
Look below and you will see,
It is...

Answer: A unicorn.

May Sonsthagen (4)
Arundel CE Primary School, Arundel

Tahlia's First Riddle

What could it be?
Follow the clues and see.

It looks like **a pony**.
It sounds like ***clip, clop***.
It smells like **sugar**.
It feels like **a soft pillow**.
It tastes like **marshmallows**.

Have you guessed what it could be?
Look below and you will see,
It is...

Answer: A unicorn.

Tahlia Aston (4)
Arundel CE Primary School, Arundel

Ella's First Riddle

What could it be?
Follow the clues and see.

It looks like **a rainbow**.
It sounds like *clip, clop*.
It smells like **chocolate**.
It feels like **a pillow**.
It tastes like **sweeties**.

Have you guessed what it could be?
Look below and you will see,
It is...

Answer: A unicorn.

Ella Slade (4)
Arundel CE Primary School, Arundel

Zayn's First Riddle

What could it be?
Follow the clues and see.

It looks like **a brown cushion**.
It sounds like **a monkey**.
It smells like **bananas**.
It feels like **fluff**.
It tastes like **bananas**.

Have you guessed what it could be?
Look below and you will see,
It is...

Answer: A monkey.

Zayn Keane (4)
Arundel CE Primary School, Arundel

Tyreece's First Riddle

What could it be?
Follow the clues and see.

It looks like **a branch**.
It sounds like **sss**.
It smells like **wood**.
It feels like **smooth wood**.
It tastes like **slime**.

Have you guessed what it could be?
Look below and you will see,
It is...

Answer: A snake.

Tyreece Ford (5)
Arundel CE Primary School, Arundel

Max's First Riddle

What could it be?
Follow the clues and see.

It looks like **a lollipop**.
It sounds like **a roar**.
It smells like **a lollipop**.
It feels like **a cushion**.
It tastes like **meat**.

Have you guessed what it could be?
Look below and you will see,
It is...

Answer: A T-rex.

Max Withall (5)
Arundel CE Primary School, Arundel

Douglas' First Riddle

What could it be?
Follow the clues and see.

It looks like **a red tower**.
It sounds like **fire**.
It smells like **smoke**.
It feels like **a dragon**.
It tastes like **meat**.

Have you guessed what it could be?
Look below and you will see,
It is...

Answer: A dragon.

Douglas Pacey (5)
Arundel CE Primary School, Arundel

Riley's First Riddle

Who could it be?
Follow the clues and see.

He has **pointy ears on his head**.
He has **a deep voice**.
He smells like **a bat**.
He feels like **a cape**.
He tastes like **a bat**.

Have you guessed who it could be?
Look below and you will see,
It is…

Answer: Batman.

Riley Hummerstone (4)
Arundel CE Primary School, Arundel

Oscar's First Riddle

What could it be?
Follow the clues and see.

It looks like **soft sand**.
It sounds like *crunch, crunch*.
It smells like **the sea**.
It feels like **soft sand**.
It tastes like **ice cream**.

Have you guessed what it could be?
Look below and you will see,
It is...

Answer: *The beach.*

Oscar Eacott-May (4)
Audley Primary School, Caterham

Maia's First Riddle

What could it be?
Follow the clues and see.

It looks like **a sunny day**.
It sounds like **children playing**.
It smells like **seaweed**.
It feels like **soft sand**.
It tastes like **fish and chips**.

Have you guessed what it could be?
Look below and you will see,
It is...

Answer: *The beach.*

Maia Quarmby (5)
Audley Primary School, Caterham

Tommy's First Riddle

What could it be?
Follow the clues and see.

It looks like **waves**.
It sounds like **children playing**.
It smells like **fish and chips**.
It feels like **warm sand**.
It tastes like **salty water**.

Have you guessed what it could be?
Look below and you will see,
It is...

Answer: *The beach.*

Tommy Pendino (5)
Audley Primary School, Caterham

Eli's First Riddle

What could it be?
Follow the clues and see.

It looks like **a sunny day**.
It sounds like **seagulls**.
It smells like **ice cream**.
It feels like **hot sand**.
It tastes like **fish and chips**.

Have you guessed what it could be?
Look below and you will see,
It is…

Answer: *The beach.*

Eli Pocock (5)
Audley Primary School, Caterham

Henry's First Riddle

What could it be?
Follow the clues and see.

It looks like **a sunny day**.
It sounds like **waves**.
It smells like **salty water**.
It feels like **soft sand**.
It tastes like **fish and chips**.

Have you guessed what it could be?
Look below and you will see,
It is...

Answer: *The beach.*

Henry Downs (5)
Audley Primary School, Caterham

Hannah's First Riddle

What could it be?
Follow the clues and see.

It looks like **glistening sand**.
It sounds like **waves crashing**.
It smells like **ice cream**.
It feels **warm**.
It tastes like **salty water**.

Have you guessed what it could be?
Look below and you will see,
It is...

Answer: *The beach.*

Hannah Scourfield (5)
Audley Primary School, Caterham

Harrison's First Riddle

What could it be?
Follow the clues and see.

It looks like **sunshine**.
It sounds like **splashing water**.
It smells like **seaweed**.
It feels like **sand**.
It tastes like **the salty sea**.

Have you guessed what it could be?
Look below and you will see,
It is...

Answer: *The beach.*

Harrison Bennett (4)
Audley Primary School, Caterham

Zayn's First Riddle

What could it be?
Follow the clues and see.

It looks like **a sunny day**.
It sounds like **fun**.
It smells like **fish and chips**.
It feels like **soft sand**.
It tastes like **ice cream**.

Have you guessed what it could be?
Look below and you will see,
It is...

Answer: *The beach.*

Zayn Uddin (4)
Audley Primary School, Caterham

Ethan's First Riddle

What could it be?
Follow the clues and see.

It looks **sunny**.
It sounds like *splash*.
It smells like **shells**.
It feels like **sand**.
It tastes like **salty water**.

Have you guessed what it could be?
Look below and you will see,
It is...

Answer: *The beach.*

Ethan Sherriff (5)
Audley Primary School, Caterham

Jake's First Riddle

What could it be?
Follow the clues and see.

It looks like **boats in the sea**.
It sounds **wavy**.
It smells like **salty sand**.
It feels like **soft sand**.
It tastes like **ice cream**.

Have you guessed what it could be?
Look below and you will see,
It is...

Answer: The beach.

Jake Quarmby (5)
Audley Primary School, Caterham

Charlie's First Riddle

What could it be?
Follow the clues and see.

It looks like **the blue sky**.
It sounds like **children playing**.
It smells like **fish and chips**.
It feels **sandy**.
It tastes **salty**.

Have you guessed what it could be?
Look below and you will see,
It is...

Answer: *The beach.*

Charlie Lewis Mons (5)
Audley Primary School, Caterham

Jack's First Riddle

What could it be?
Follow the clues and see.

It looks like **the sand**.
It sounds like **children playing**.
It smells like **waves**.
It feels like **soft sand**.
It tastes like **salt**.

Have you guessed what it could be?
Look below and you will see,
It is...

Answer: *The beach.*

Jack Gittins (4)
Audley Primary School, Caterham

Lois' First Riddle

What could it be?
Follow the clues and see.

It looks like **fun**.
It sounds like **seagulls**.
It smells like **ice cream**.
It feels like **soft sand**.
It tastes like **salty water**.

Have you guessed what it could be?
Look below and you will see,
It is...

Answer: The beach.

Lois Elsley (5)
Audley Primary School, Caterham

Cohen's First Riddle

What could it be?
Follow the clues and see.

It looks like **rocks falling**.
It sounds like **splashing**.
It smells like **water**.
It feels like **soft sand**.
It tastes like **salt**.

Have you guessed what it could be?
Look below and you will see,
It is...

Answer: *The beach.*

Cohen Wright (4)
Audley Primary School, Caterham

Isla's First Riddle

What could it be?
Follow the clues and see.

It looks like **waves**.
It sounds like **seagulls**.
It smells like **ice cream**.
It feels like **crunchy sand**.
It tastes like **salt**.

Have you guessed what it could be?
Look below and you will see,
It is...

Answer: *The beach.*

Isla Reynolds (4)
Audley Primary School, Caterham

Sebastian's First Riddle

What could it be?
Follow the clues and see.

It looks like **soft sand**.
It sounds like **splashing**.
It smells like **salt**.
It feels **soft**.
It tastes like **cheese sandwiches**.

Have you guessed what it could be?
Look below and you will see,
It is...

Answer: The beach.

Sebastian Mansfield (4)
Audley Primary School, Caterham

Emilia's First Riddle

What could it be?
Follow the clues and see.

It looks like **waves**.
It sounds like **seagulls**.
It smells like **seaweed**.
It feels like **soft sand**.
It tastes like **hot dogs**.

Have you guessed what it could be?
Look below and you will see,
It is...

Answer: *The beach.*

Emilia Bontas (5)
Audley Primary School, Caterham

Amy's First Riddle

What could it be?
Follow the clues and see.

It looks like **a sunny day**.
It sounds like **boats**.
It smells like **wet sand**.
It feels **warm**.
It tastes like **ice cream**.

Have you guessed what it could be?
Look below and you will see,
It is...

Answer: *The beach.*

Amy May Beck (4)
Audley Primary School, Caterham

Robbie's First Riddle

What could it be?
Follow the clues and see.

It looks like **sand**.
It sounds like **splashing**.
It smells like **fish**.
It feels like **summer**.
It tastes like **peanut butter**.

Have you guessed what it could be?
Look below and you will see,
It is...

Answer: *The beach.*

Robbie Seal (5)
Audley Primary School, Caterham

Sophia's First Riddle

What could it be?
Follow the clues and see.

It looks like **the sun**.
It sounds like **fun**.
It smells like **ice cream**.
It feels like **warm sand**.
It tastes like **seaweed**.

Have you guessed what it could be?
Look below and you will see,
It is...

Answer: The beach.

Sophia Myrmus (5)
Audley Primary School, Caterham

Zion's First Riddle

What could it be?
Follow the clues and see.

It looks like **waves**.
It sounds like **whales**.
It smells like **sand**.
It feels like **soft sand**.
It tastes like **salty water**.

Have you guessed what it could be?
Look below and you will see,
It is...

Answer: The beach.

Zion Edwards (4)
Audley Primary School, Caterham

Charlie's First Riddle

What could it be?
Follow the clues and see.

It looks like **sunshine**.
It sounds like **waves**.
It smells like **sand**.
It feels like **wet water**.
It tastes like **hot dogs**.

Have you guessed what it could be?
Look below and you will see,
It is...

Answer: *The beach.*

Charlie Cox (4)
Audley Primary School, Caterham

Eryn's First Riddle

What could it be?
Follow the clues and see.

It looks like **sand**.
It sounds like **seagulls**.
It smells like **seaweed**.
It feels like **salty sand**.
It tastes like **chips**.

Have you guessed what it could be?
Look below and you will see,
It is...

Answer: The beach.

Eryn Llewellyn Bayliss (4)
Audley Primary School, Caterham

Michael's First Riddle

What could it be?
Follow the clues and see.

It looks **sandy**.
It sounds like **waves**.
It smells like **seaweed**.
It feels like **hot sand**.
It tastes like **salty chips**.

Have you guessed what it could be?
Look below and you will see,
It is...

Answer: *The beach.*

Michael Deiana (5)
Audley Primary School, Caterham

Pearse's First Riddle

What could it be?
Follow the clues and see.

It looks like **the sea**.
It sounds like **boats**.
It smells like **food**.
It feels like **soft sand**.
It tastes like **sugar**.

Have you guessed what it could be?
Look below and you will see,
It is...

Answer: *The beach.*

Pearse Lewis (5)
Audley Primary School, Caterham

Sienna's First Riddle

What could it be?
Follow the clues and see.

It looks like **a sunny day**.
It sounds like **fun**.
It smells like **seaweed**.
It feels like **sand**.
It tastes like **salt**.

Have you guessed what it could be?
Look below and you will see,
It is...

Answer: *The beach.*

Sienna Smith (5)
Audley Primary School, Caterham

Beatrice's First Riddle

What could it be?
Follow the clues and see.

It looks like **sand**.
It sounds **wavy**.
It smells like **seaweed**.
It feels like **warm sand**.
It tastes like **ice cream**.

Have you guessed what it could be?
Look below and you will see,
It is...

Answer: *The beach.*

Beatrice Ramsey (4)
Audley Primary School, Caterham

Phoebe's First Riddle

What could it be?
Follow the clues and see.

It looks like **sand**.
It sounds like **the sea**.
It smells **hot**.
It feels like **wet sand**.
It tastes like **salt**.

Have you guessed what it could be?
Look below and you will see,
It is...

Answer: *The beach*.

Phoebe Hayman (4)
Audley Primary School, Caterham

Louie's First Riddle

What could it be?
Follow the clues and see.

It looks like **hot sand**.
It sounds like **waves**.
It smells like **salt**.
It feels **hot**.
It tastes like **water**.

Have you guessed what it could be?
Look below and you will see,
It is...

Answer: *The beach.*

Louie Gillespie (4)
Audley Primary School, Caterham

Morganna's First Riddle

What could it be?
Follow the clues and see.

It looks like **the sand**.
It sounds like **shells**.
It smells like **seaweed**.
It feels **hot**.
It tastes **salty**.

Have you guessed what it could be?
Look below and you will see,
It is...

Answer: The beach.

Morganna Evans (4)
Audley Primary School, Caterham

Jasmine's First Riddle

What could it be?
Follow the clues and see.

It looks like **a glossy, milky, dark brown slab.**
It sounds like **a snap and crunch.**
It smells like **a sweet, aromatic and rich scent.**
It feels like **velvet melting on my tongue and squishy cuddles.**
It tastes **yummy and delicious.**

Have you guessed what it could be?
Look below and you will see,
It is...

Answer: Chocolate.

Jasmine Sandhu (5)
Brighton College Nursery, Pre-Prep And Prep School, Brighton

Aryav's First Riddle

What could it be?
Follow the clues and see.

It looks like **a metal box with glass windows**.
It sounds like *vroom, vroom*.
It smells like **diesel**.
It feels **cosy inside**.
It tastes like **metal**.

Have you guessed what it could be?
Look below and you will see,
It is...

Answer: A car.

Aryav Clitus (5)
Brighton College Nursery, Pre-Prep And Prep School, Brighton

Laurence's First Riddle

What could it be?
Follow the clues and see.

It looks like **a shiny castle**.
It sounds **wibbly wobbly**.
It smells like **fruit lollipops**.
It feels like **cold slime**.
It tastes like **yummy strawberries**.

Have you guessed what it could be?
Look below and you will see,
It is...

Answer: Jelly.

Laurence Fox (5)
Brighton College Nursery, Pre-Prep And Prep School, Brighton

Amaury's First Riddle

What could it be?
Follow the clues and see.

It looks like **worms**.
It sounds like *slurp, slurp*.
It smells like **Italy**.
It feels **squidgy and slimy**.
It tastes like **tomatoes**.

Have you guessed what it could be?
Look below and you will see,
It is...

Answer: Spaghetti bolognese.

Amaury David Rowe-Roberts (5)
Brighton College Nursery, Pre-Prep And Prep School, Brighton

Elizabeth's First Riddle

What could it be?
Follow the clues and see.

It looks like **water**.
It sounds like *pss, pss*.
It smells like **wet flowers**.
It feels **cold**.
It tastes like **clouds**.

Have you guessed what it could be?
Look below and you will see,
It is...

Answer: *Rain*.

Elizabeth Rosa Oliveri (4)
Brighton College Nursery, Pre-Prep And Prep School, Brighton

Ariana's First Riddle

What could it be?
Follow the clues and see.

It looks like **the colour red**.
It sounds **crunchy and crispy**.
It smells **fresh and ripe**.
It feels like **a hard ball**.
It tastes **juicy and sweet**.

Have you guessed what it could be?
Look below and you will see,
It is...

Answer: A red apple.

Ariana Keely (4)
Brighton College Nursery, Pre-Prep And Prep School, Brighton

Alexander's First Riddle

What could it be?
Follow the clues and see.

It looks like **a six-pointed thing**.
It sounds like **twinkle, twinkle**.
It smells like **night-time air**.
It feels like **a wand**.
It tastes like **glitter**.

Have you guessed what it could be?
Look below and you will see,
It is...

Answer: A star.

Alexander Putra Downes-Yusuf (5)
Brighton College Nursery, Pre-Prep And Prep School, Brighton

Zak's First Riddle

What could it be?
Follow the clues and see.

It looks like **a reflection of the sky**.
It sounds like **waves crashing**.
It smells like **seaweed**.
It feels like **a cold bath**.
It tastes like **salt**.

Have you guessed what it could be?
Look below and you will see,
It is...

Answer: *The sea.*

Zak Helalat (4)
Brighton College Nursery, Pre-Prep And Prep School, Brighton

Maia's First Riddle

What could it be?
Follow the clues and see.

It looks like **a fluffy ball**.
It sounds like **a creaky door**.
It smells like **a bunny**.
It feels like **a soft pillow**.
It tastes like **a teddy bear**.

Have you guessed what it could be?
Look below and you will see,
It is...

Answer: *A kitten.*

Maia Warren-Lewis (4)
Brighton College Nursery, Pre-Prep And Prep School, Brighton

Eden's First Riddle

What could it be?
Follow the clues and see.

It looks like **a machine**.
It sounds like **broken metal**.
It smells like **a computer**.
It feels like **a car door**.
It tastes like **a tin can**.

Have you guessed what it could be?
Look below and you will see,
It is…

Answer: A robot.

Eden Warren-Lewis (4)
Brighton College Nursery, Pre-Prep And Prep School, Brighton

Jaclyn's First Riddle

What could it be?
Follow the clues and see.

It looks like **a bird**.
It sounds like *gawk, gawk*.
It smells like **the sea**.
It feels like **fluffy toys**.
It tastes like **fish**.

Have you guessed what it could be?
Look below and you will see,
It is...

Answer: A penguin.

Jaclyn Yap (4)
Brighton College Nursery, Pre-Prep And Prep School, Brighton

Jake's First Riddle

What could it be?
Follow the clues and see.

It looks **black and white**.
It sounds like **a noisy bird**.
It smells like **fish**.
It feels **soft and smooth**.
It tastes like **salty water**.

Have you guessed what it could be?
Look below and you will see,
It is...

Answer: A penguin.

Jake Munslow (5)
Brighton College Nursery, Pre-Prep And Prep School, Brighton

Shu Yuan's First Riddle

What could it be?
Follow the clues and see.

It looks like **an animal**.
It sounds like *puff, puff*.
It smells like **cotton**.
It feels **fluffy**.
It tastes like **nothing**.

Have you guessed what it could be?
Look below and you will see,
It is...

Answer: A teddy bear.

Shu Yuan Wang (5)
Brighton College Nursery, Pre-Prep And Prep School, Brighton

Ellen's First Riddle

What could it be?
Follow the clues and see.

It looks like **a white block**.
It sounds like *plop, plop*.
It smells like **soy sauce**.
It feels like **silk**.
It tastes like **milk**.

Have you guessed what it could be?
Look below and you will see,
It is...

Answer: Tofu.

Ellen Xu (5)
Brighton College Nursery, Pre-Prep And Prep School, Brighton

Arjun's First Riddle

What could it be?
Follow the clues and see.

It looks like **a man with a helmet**.
It sounds like **a light**.
It smells like **armour**.
It feels **hard and cold**.
It tastes like **rust**.

Have you guessed what it could be?
Look below and you will see,
It is...

Answer: A knight.

Arjun Balakrishnan Banani (4)
Brighton College Nursery, Pre-Prep And Prep School, Brighton

Annabel's First Riddle

What could it be?
Follow the clues and see.

It looks like **a comet**.
It sounds like **crackle and pop**.
It smells like **sugar**.
It feels like **a sponge**.
It tastes like **candy**.

Have you guessed what it could be?
Look below and you will see,
It is...

Answer: Popcorn.

Annabel Elizabeth Downes-Yusuf (5)
Brighton College Nursery, Pre-Prep And Prep School, Brighton

Aiden's First Riddle

What could it be?
Follow the clues and see.

It looks like **a man**.
It sounds like **a machine**.
It smells like **nothing**.
It feels like **something cold**.
It tastes like **metal**.

Have you guessed what it could be?
Look below and you will see,
It is...

Answer: A robot.

Aiden Chowdhury (4)
Brighton College Nursery, Pre-Prep And Prep School, Brighton

Eden's First Riddle

What could it be?
Follow the clues and see.

It looks like **a pony**.
It sounds like **angels**.
It smells like **clouds**.
It feels like **soft wool**.
It tastes like **sweets**.

Have you guessed what it could be?
Look below and you will see,
It is...

Answer: A unicorn.

Eden Raiss (4)
Brighton College Nursery, Pre-Prep And Prep School, Brighton

Zach's First Riddle

What could it be?
Follow the clues and see.

It looks **pretty**.
It sounds like **the wind**.
It smells like **Mummy**.
It feels like **soft foam**.
It tastes like **bamboo**.

Have you guessed what it could be?
Look below and you will see,
It is...

Answer: A flower.

Zach Field (4)
Brighton College Nursery, Pre-Prep And Prep School, Brighton

Aoife's First Riddle

What could it be?
Follow the clues and see.

It looks like **a furry monster**.
It sounds like **a loud dinosaur**.
It smells like **a crunchy bone**.
It feels like **a soft couch**.
It tastes like **a mouth of fur**.

Have you guessed what it could be?
Look below and you will see,
It is...

Answer: A dog.

Aoife Cassell (5)
Broadwater CE Primary School, Worthing

Wilfred's First Riddle

What could it be?
Follow the clues and see.

It looks like **a giraffe**.
It sounds like **a lawnmower**.
It smells like **a rotten egg**.
It feels like **a hard, bony thing**.
It tastes like **a rotten dragon**.

Have you guessed what it could be?
Look below and you will see,
It is...

Answer: A dinosaur.

Wilfred Oscar Miles (4)
Broadwater CE Primary School, Worthing

Sophie's First Riddle

What could it be?
Follow the clues and see.

It looks like **a giant rock**.
It sounds like **a tiger's roar**.
It smells like **stinky eggs**.
It feels like **rough trees**.
It tastes like **horrid breath**.

Have you guessed what it could be?
Look below and you will see,
It is...

Answer: A dinosaur.

Sophie Hollisey-McLean (5)
Broadwater CE Primary School, Worthing

Ella's First Riddle

What could it be?
Follow the clues and see.

It looks like **a rock**.
It sounds like *squeak, squeak*.
It smells like **lettuce**.
It feels like **a soft pillow**.
It tastes like **green grass**.

Have you guessed what it could be?
Look below and you will see,
It is...

Answer: A guinea pig.

Ella Roberts (4)
Broadwater CE Primary School, Worthing

Ava's First Riddle

What could it be?
Follow the clues and see.

It looks like **a cuddly rabbit**.
It sounds like **a puppy crying**.
It smells like **a carrot**.
It feels like **a soft hamster**.
It tastes like **yummy grass**.

Have you guessed what it could be?
Look below and you will see,
It is…

Answer: A rabbit.

Ava van der Mark (4)
Broadwater CE Primary School, Worthing

Ellis' First Riddle

What could it be?
Follow the clues and see.

It looks like **a slimy, green bandage**.
It sounds like **hissing**.
It smells like **a brown mouse**.
It feels like **slime**.
It tastes like **scary spaghetti**.

Have you guessed what it could be?
Look below and you will see,
It is...

Answer: A snake.

Ellis Tricker (5)
Broadwater CE Primary School, Worthing

Olivia's First Riddle

What could it be?
Follow the clues and see.

It looks like **a golden toy**.
It sounds like **bubble, bubble**.
It smells like **salt**.
It feels like **a slippery duck**.
It tastes like **a chicken**.

Have you guessed what it could be?
Look below and you will see,
It is...

Answer: *A fish*.

Olivia Jenner McWilton (5)
Broadwater CE Primary School, Worthing

Ava's First Riddle

What could it be?
Follow the clues and see.

It looks like **a house**.
It sounds like **an elephant**.
It smells like **a stinky fish**.
It feels like **a spiky hedgehog**.
It tastes like **a rotten egg**.

Have you guessed what it could be?
Look below and you will see,
It is...

Answer: A dinosaur.

Ava Sparkes (4)
Broadwater CE Primary School, Worthing

Lucas' First Riddle

What could it be?
Follow the clues and see.

It looks like **a tall giraffe**.
It sounds like **fireworks**.
It smells like **stinky fish**.
It feels like **hard bricks**.
It tastes like **worms on toast**.

Have you guessed what it could be?
Look below and you will see,
It is...

Answer: A dinosaur.

Lucas Peckham (4)
Broadwater CE Primary School, Worthing

Ethan's First Riddle

What could it be?
Follow the clues and see.

It looks like **a monster truck**.
It sounds like **an engine**.
It smells like **a stinky poo**.
It feels like **a snake**.
It tastes like **disgusting meat**.

Have you guessed what it could be?
Look below and you will see,
It is...

Answer: A dinosaur.

Ethan Welikele (5)
Broadwater CE Primary School, Worthing

Darwyn's First Riddle

What could it be?
Follow the clues and see.

It looks like **a tank**.
It sounds like **a lion**.
It smells like **a stinky bug**.
It feels like **heavy, metal armour**.
It tastes like **rotten tomatoes**.

Have you guessed what it could be?
Look below and you will see,
It is...

Answer: A dinosaur.

Darwyn Raine Buller (5)
Broadwater CE Primary School, Worthing

Alice's First Riddle

What could it be?
Follow the clues and see.

It looks like **a small rock**.
It sounds like **squeak, squeak**.
It smells like **cheese**.
It feels like **a soft coat**.
It tastes like **whiskers**.

Have you guessed what it could be?
Look below and you will see,
It is...

Answer: A mouse.

Alice Monk (4)
Broadwater CE Primary School, Worthing

Elliot's First Riddle

What could it be?
Follow the clues and see.

It looks like **a green leaf**.
It sounds like *slither, slither*.
It smells like **slime**.
It feels like **slippery water**.
It tastes like **mice**.

Have you guessed what it could be?
Look below and you will see,
It is...

Answer: A snake.

Elliot Samuel Smith (4)
Broadwater CE Primary School, Worthing

Bebe's First Riddle

What could it be?
Follow the clues and see.

It looks like **a soft cushion**.
It sounds like *click, clock*.
It smells like **a fish**.
It feels like **a comfy coat**.
It tastes like **milky fur**.

Have you guessed what it could be?
Look below and you will see,
It is...

Answer: A cat.

Bebe Stratten (5)
Broadwater CE Primary School, Worthing

Otto's First Riddle

What could it be?
Follow the clues and see.

It looks like **a fluffy pillow**.
It sounds like **a thirsty boy**.
It smells like **a hard bone**.
It feels like **a soft teddy**.
It tastes like **hairy fluff**.

Have you guessed what it could be?
Look below and you will see,
It is...

Answer: A dog.

Otto George-Holgate (5)
Broadwater CE Primary School, Worthing

Stanley's First Riddle

What could it be?
Follow the clues and see.

It looks like **a flying superhero**.
It sounds like **tweet, tweet**.
It smells like **small seeds**.
It feels like **my hair**.
It tastes like **nuts**.

Have you guessed what it could be?
Look below and you will see,
It is...

Answer: A bird.

Stanley Robert Spencer (5)
Broadwater CE Primary School, Worthing

Seth's First Riddle

What could it be?
Follow the clues and see.

It looks like **a house**.
It sounds like **an elephant**.
It smells like **stinky fish**.
It feels like **a spiky hedgehog**.
It tastes like **a rotten egg**.

Have you guessed what it could be?
Look below and you will see,
It is...

Answer: A dinosaur.

Seth Martin (5)
Broadwater CE Primary School, Worthing

Stanley's First Riddle

What could it be?
Follow the clues and see.

It looks like **a snake**.
It sounds like **blowing raspberries**.
It smells like **the ground**.
It feels like **bumpy rocks**.
It tastes like **buzzy flies**.

Have you guessed what it could be?
Look below and you will see,
It is...

Answer: A lizard.

Stanley Laycock (4)
Broadwater CE Primary School, Worthing

Liam's First Riddle

What could it be?
Follow the clues and see.

It looks like **a hopping rock**.
It sounds like **shaking maracas**.
It smells like **a carrot**.
It feels like **a soft toy**.
It tastes like **green grass**.

Have you guessed what it could be?
Look below and you will see,
It is...

Answer: A rabbit.

Liam Condon (5)
Broadwater CE Primary School, Worthing

Thomas' First Riddle

What could it be?
Follow the clues and see.

It looks like **a shiny orange**.
It sounds like **bubbles blowing**.
It smells like **silver water**.
It feels like **slippery rain**.
It tastes like **a tank**.

Have you guessed what it could be?
Look below and you will see,
It is...

Answer: A fish.

Thomas Rogers (4)
Broadwater CE Primary School, Worthing

Judith's First Riddle

What could it be?
Follow the clues and see.

It looks like **a hairball**.
It sounds like **a squeaky toy**.
It smells like **biscuits**.
It feels like **a soft hat**.
It tastes like **a crunchy carrot**.

Have you guessed what it could be?
Look below and you will see,
It is…

Answer: A hamster.

Judith Emerson (5)
Broadwater CE Primary School, Worthing

Ella's First Riddle

What could it be?
Follow the clues and see.

It looks like **a big rock**.
It sounds like **a monster**.
It smells like **fire and smoke**.
It feels like **a hard wall**.
It tastes like **stinky eggs**.

Have you guessed what it could be?
Look below and you will see,
It is...

Answer: A dinosaur.

Ella Kinnear (4)
Broadwater CE Primary School, Worthing

Tim's First Riddle

What could it be?
Follow the clues and see.

It looks like **a building**.
It sounds like **a hammer**.
It smells like **stinky teeth**.
It feels like **hard spikes**.
It tastes like **rotten eggs**.

Have you guessed what it could be?
Look below and you will see,
It is...

Answer: A dinosaur.

Tim Le Tian Yu (5)
Broadwater CE Primary School, Worthing

Dereks' First Riddle

What could it be?
Follow the clues and see.

It looks like **a giraffe**.
It sounds like **a tiger**.
It smells like **stinky eggs**.
It feels like **sharp sticks**.
It tastes like **a stinky fish**.

Have you guessed what it could be?
Look below and you will see,
It is...

Answer: A dinosaur.

Dereks Lazdans (5)
Broadwater CE Primary School, Worthing

Dylan's First Riddle

What could it be?
Follow the clues and see.

It looks like **a fluffy toy**.
It sounds like **children crying**.
It smells like **fur**.
It feels like **a snuggly pillow**.
It tastes like **yummy fish**.

Have you guessed what it could be?
Look below and you will see,
It is...

Answer: A cat.

Dylan Thompson (4)
Broadwater CE Primary School, Worthing

Layla's First Riddle

What could it be?
Follow the clues and see.

It looks like **a long tank**.
It sounds like **a stomp**.
It smells like **rotten fish**.
It feels like **hard bricks**.
It tastes like **smelly fish**.

Have you guessed what it could be?
Look below and you will see,
It is...

Answer: A dinosaur.

Layla Crystal Gadsby-Pullen (5)
Broadwater CE Primary School, Worthing

Noah's First Riddle

What could it be?
Follow the clues and see.

It looks like **a giraffe**.
It sounds like **a machine**.
It smells like **rotten eggs**.
It feels like **hard spikes**.
It tastes like **rotten fish**.

Have you guessed what it could be?
Look below and you will see,
It is...

Answer: A dinosaur.

Noah Wetherill (4)
Broadwater CE Primary School, Worthing

Marco's First Riddle

What could it be?
Follow the clues and see.

It looks like **brown mud**.
It sounds like *ruff, ruff*.
It smells like **the grass**.
It feels like **a soft pillow**.
It tastes like **bones**.

Have you guessed what it could be?
Look below and you will see,
It is...

Answer: A dog.

Marco Li (6)
Broadwater CE Primary School, Worthing

Reuben's First Riddle

What could it be?
Follow the clues and see.

It looks like **a train**.
It sounds like **a hard hammer**.
It smells like **rotten eggs**.
It feels like **a hard wall**.
It tastes like **bad veg**.

Have you guessed what it could be?
Look below and you will see,
It is...

Answer: A dinosaur.

Reuben Thomas (4)
Broadwater CE Primary School, Worthing

Joel's First Riddle

What could it be?
Follow the clues and see.

It looks like **a fluffy pillow**.
It sounds like **a baby crying**.
It smells like **fish**.
It feels like **a cuddly toy**.
It tastes like **good milk**.

Have you guessed what it could be?
Look below and you will see,
It is...

Answer: A cat.

Joel Powell-Staggs (4)
Broadwater CE Primary School, Worthing

Samuel's First Riddle

What could it be?
Follow the clues and see.

It looks like **a bulldozer**.
It sounds like **a big hammer**.
It smells like **stinky eggs**.
It feels like **a wall**.
It tastes like **bad fish**.

Have you guessed what it could be?
Look below and you will see,
It is...

Answer: A dinosaur.

Samuel Croft (4)
Broadwater CE Primary School, Worthing

Raife's First Riddle

What could it be?
Follow the clues and see.

It looks like **a fluffy ball**.
It sounds like *miaow, miaow*.
It smells like **fish**.
It feels like **a soft toy**.
It tastes like **milk**.

Have you guessed what it could be?
Look below and you will see,
It is...

Answer: A cat.

Raife Bird (4)
Broadwater CE Primary School, Worthing

Jack's First Riddle

What could it be?
Follow the clues and see.

It looks like **a brown tree**.
It sounds like *ruff, ruff*.
It smells like **cheese**.
It feels like **fur**.
It tastes like **furry sugar**.

Have you guessed what it could be?
Look below and you will see,
It is...

Answer: A dog.

Jack Spicer (4)
Broadwater CE Primary School, Worthing

Seb's First Riddle

What could it be?
Follow the clues and see.

It looks like **a soft pillow**.
It sounds like **a monster crying**.
It smells like **a fish**.
It feels like **a cuddly toy**.
It tastes like **milk**.

Have you guessed what it could be?
Look below and you will see,
It is...

Answer: A cat.

Seb Sparkes (4)
Broadwater CE Primary School, Worthing

Charlie's First Riddle

What could it be?
Follow the clues and see.

It looks like **a crane**.
It sounds like **a drill**.
It smells like **a stinky egg**.
It feels like **hard bone**.
It tastes like **mouldy fish**.

Have you guessed what it could be?
Look below and you will see,
It is...

Answer: A *dinosaur.*

Charlie Scrase (4)
Broadwater CE Primary School, Worthing

Hendrix's First Riddle

What could it be?
Follow the clues and see.

It looks like **a giant**.
It sounds like **an elephant**.
It smells like **stinky eggs**.
It feels like **bones**.
It tastes like **horrid eggs**.

Have you guessed what it could be?
Look below and you will see,
It is...

Answer: A dinosaur.

Hendrix Batchelor-Kent (4)
Broadwater CE Primary School, Worthing

Lottie's First Riddle

What could it be?
Follow the clues and see.

It looks like **a car**.
It sounds like **an elephant**.
It smells like **stinky eggs**.
It feels like **a car**.
It tastes like **rotten eggs**.

Have you guessed what it could be?
Look below and you will see,
It is...

Answer: A dinosaur.

Lottie Olivia Bell (4)
Broadwater CE Primary School, Worthing

Jaxson's First Riddle

What could it be?
Follow the clues and see.

It looks like **gold**.
It sounds like **bubbles**.
It smells like **fish and chips**.
It feels like **wet water**.
It tastes like **the sea**.

Have you guessed what it could be?
Look below and you will see,
It is...

Answer: A fish.

Jaxson Hughes (4)
Broadwater CE Primary School, Worthing

Mia's First Riddle

What could it be?
Follow the clues and see.

It looks like **a teardrop**.
It sounds like *pitter, patter*.
It smells like **soil**.
It feels **cold**.
It tastes like **metal**.

Have you guessed what it could be?
Look below and you will see,
It is...

Answer: *Rain*.

Mia Pearson (4)
Chyngton Primary School, Seaford

Harry's First Riddle

What could it be?
Follow the clues and see.

It looks like **a long tube**.
It sounds like *choo, choo*.
It smells like **electricity on the tracks**.
It feels like **metal**.
It tastes like **dirt**.

Have you guessed what it could be?
Look below and you will see,
It is...

Answer: A train.

Harry Whittington (4)
Essendene Lodge School, Caterham

Sadie's First Riddle

What could it be?
Follow the clues and see.

It looks like **a queen**.
It sounds like **beautiful singing**.
It smells like **flowers**.
It feels **smooth like cream**.
It tastes like **sweeties**.

Have you guessed what it could be?
Look below and you will see,
It is...

Answer: A princess.

Sadie Vernon (4)
Essendene Lodge School, Caterham

Calum's First Riddle

What could they be?
Follow the clues and see.

They have **an eyepatch**.
They sound like **ahoy**.
They smell like **smelly socks**.
They feel **skinny**.
They taste **disgusting**.

Have you guessed what they could be?
Look below and you will see,
They are...

Answer: Pirates.

Calum Grippman (5)
Essendene Lodge School, Caterham

Harvey's First Riddle

What could it be?
Follow the clues and see.

It looks like **a lizard**.
It sounds like **a roar**.
It smells like **it is cold**.
It feels like **scales**.
It tastes like **fresh meat**.

Have you guessed what it could be?
Look below and you will see,
It is...

Answer: A dinosaur.

Harvey Vigor-Messenger (5)
Essendene Lodge School, Caterham

Teddy's First Riddle

What could it be?
Follow the clues and see.

It has **two handles**.
It sounds like **broom, broom.**
It smells like **gas**.
It feels like **a car**.
It tastes like **metal**.

Have you guessed what it could be?
Look below and you will see,
It is...

Answer: A motorbike.

Teddy Scarffe (4)
Essendene Lodge School, Caterham

Isabella's First Riddle

What could it be?
Follow the clues and see.

It looks like **a fish**.
It sounds like **singing**.
It smells like **the sea**.
It feels **slippery**.
It tastes like **a fish**.

Have you guessed what it could be?
Look below and you will see,
It is…

Answer: A mermaid.

Isabella Ndumiyana (5)
Essendene Lodge School, Caterham

Eveleigh's First Riddle

What could it be?
Follow the clues and see.

It has **wings**.
It sounds like **fluttering**.
It smells like **vanilla**.
It feels **smooth**.
It tastes like **fairy dust**.

Have you guessed what it could be?
Look below and you will see,
It is...

Answer: A fairy.

Eveleigh Sutton (5)
Kew Riverside Primary School, Richmond

Vasco's First Riddle

What could it be?
Follow the clues and see.

It looks like **a human**.
It sounds **quiet**.
It smells **stinky**.
It feels **soft**.
It tastes like **the enemy**.

Have you guessed what it could be?
Look below and you will see,
It is...

Answer: A ninja.

Vasco Ramos (5)
Kew Riverside Primary School, Richmond

Yuv's First Riddle

What could it be?
Follow the clues and see.

It looks like **a brown phone**.
It sounds like **yum, yum**.
It smells like **milk**.
It feels **hard, but it's soft when kept in the sun**.
It tastes **sweet, like honey**.

Have you guessed what it could be?
Look below and you will see,
It is...

Answer: Chocolate.

Yuv Desai (5)
Krishna Avanti Primary School, Croydon

Eva's First Riddle

What could it be?
Follow the clues and see.

It looks like **a cloud**.
It sounds like **a balloon popping**.
It smells like **butter**.
It feels like **sheep's wool**.
It tastes like **something salty**.

Have you guessed what it could be?
Look below and you will see,
It is...

Answer: Popcorn.

Eva Desai (5)
Krishna Avanti Primary School, Croydon

Vihaan's First Riddle

What could it be?
Follow the clues and see.

It looks **round and swirly**.
It sounds **yummy**.
It smells like **strawberries**.
It feels **soft and squishy**.
It tastes **sweet**.

Have you guessed what it could be?
Look below and you will see,
It is...

Answer: A cupcake.

Vihaan Ravani (4)
Krishna Avanti Primary School, Croydon

Ethan's First Riddle

What could it be?
Follow the clues and see.

It looks like **a fluffy cloud**.
It sounds like **a quiet mouse**.
It smells like **yummy sweets**.
It feels like **cotton wool**.
It tastes like **sugar**.

Have you guessed what it could be?
Look below and you will see,
It is...

Answer: Candyfloss.

Ethan Penfold (4)
Northiam Primary School, Northiam

Florence's First Riddle

What could it be?
Follow the clues and see.

It looks like **green rectangles**.
It sounds like *choo, choo*.
It smells like **smoke**.
It feels **bumpy**.
It tastes like **coal**.

Have you guessed what it could be?
Look below and you will see,
It is...

Answer: A steam train.

Florence Sansom (4)
Northiam Primary School, Northiam

Olly's First Riddle

What could it be?
Follow the clues and see.

It looks like **tiny balls**.
It sounds like **rain**.
It smells like **grass**.
It feels like **sharp glass**.
It tastes like **crunchy toast**.

Have you guessed what it could be?
Look below and you will see,
It is...

Answer: Sand.

Olly Jones (5)
Northiam Primary School, Northiam

Marnie's First Riddle

What could it be?
Follow the clues and see.

It looks like **blue waves**.
It sounds like **pebbles crunching**.
It smells like **seaweed**.
It feels **wet**.
It tastes **salty**.

Have you guessed what it could be?
Look below and you will see,
It is...

Answer: The beach.

Marnie Buss (5)
Northiam Primary School, Northiam

Mariam's First Riddle

What could it be?
Follow the clues and see.

It looks like **an oval tree**.
It sounds like **a crunchy apple**.
It smells like **sweet juice**.
It feels like **a spiky hedgehog**.
It tastes like **sweet honey**.

Have you guessed what it could be?
Look below and you will see,
It is...

Answer: A pineapple.

Mariam El Mayet (5)
Notre Dame Preparatory School, Cobham

Anika's First Riddle

What could it be?
Follow the clues and see.

It is **red with seeds**.
It sounds like **a squishy**.
It smells like **a sweet flower**.
It feels like **a soft cone**.
It tastes **sweet and juicy**.

Have you guessed what it could be?
Look below and you will see,
It is...

Answer: A strawberry.

Anika Karandikar (5)
Notre Dame Preparatory School, Cobham

Agata's First Riddle

What could it be?
Follow the clues and see.

It looks like **a rugby ball**.
It sounds like **a squishy bed**.
It smells like **sweet juice**.
It feels **really hard**.
It tastes **sweet**.

Have you guessed what it could be?
Look below and you will see,
It is...

Answer: A watermelon.

Agata Muzinska (5)
Notre Dame Preparatory School, Cobham

Lucy's First Riddle

What could it be?
Follow the clues and see.

It looks like **a baby tiger**.
It sounds like *miaow.*
It smells like **fluff**.
It feels **soft**.
It tastes **yucky**.

Have you guessed what it could be?
Look below and you will see,
It is...

Answer: A pussy cat.

Lucy Jansen (4)
Reedham Park School, Purley

Max's First Riddle

What could it be?
Follow the clues and see.

It looks like **a giraffe**.
It sounds like **a roar**.
It smells like **something old**.
It feels like **a hard rock**.
It tastes like **bones**.

Have you guessed what it could be?
Look below and you will see,
It is...

Answer: A dinosaur.

Max Stock (5)
Reedham Park School, Purley

Aprayer's First Riddle

Who could it be?
Follow the clues and see.

They look like **a fairy princess**.
They sound like **weeping**.
They smell like **perfume**.
They feel **soft**.
They taste like **flowers**.

Have you guessed who it could be?
Look below and you will see,
They are...

Answer: Cinderella.

Aprayer Grant (5)
Reedham Park School, Purley

Blake's First Riddle

What could it be?
Follow the clues and see.

It looks like **yellow**.
It sounds like **peaches**.
It smells like **perfume**.
It feels **soft**.
It tastes like **flowers**.

Have you guessed what it could be?
Look below and you will see,
It is...

Answer: Beauty And The Beast.

Blake Joubert (5)
Reedham Park School, Purley

Zara's First Riddle

What could it be?
Follow the clues and see.

It looks **beautiful**.
It sounds like *neigh*.
It smells **sweet**.
It feels **soft**.
It tastes like **a rainbow**.

Have you guessed what it could be?
Look below and you will see,
It is...

Answer: A unicorn.

Zara Yasamine Anwar (4)
Reedham Park School, Purley

Isla's First Riddle

What could it be?
Follow the clues and see.

It looks like **bright and yellow with brown inside**.
It sounds like **nothing**.
It smells like **flowers and grass**.
It feels like **smooth petals and a hard middle**.
It tastes like **flowers**.

Have you guessed what it could be?
Look below and you will see,
It is...

Answer: A sunflower.

Isla Ross (4)
Send CE Primary School, Send

Fearne's First Riddle

What could it be?
Follow the clues and see.

It looks **pink and really big, it has pointy turrets.**
It sounds like **singing princesses.**
It smells like **yummy food.**
It feels **hard.**
It tastes like **candyfloss.**

Have you guessed what it could be?
Look below and you will see,
It is...

Answer: A princess' castle.

Fearne Jones (4)
Send CE Primary School, Send

Archie's First Riddle

What could it be?
Follow the clues and see.

It has **a tail and is pink and fat.**
It sounds like **a snorting noise...** *oink, oink.*
It smells like **mud.**
It feels like **rough hay.**
It tastes **disgusting.**

Have you guessed what it could be?
Look below and you will see,
It is...

Answer: A pig.

Archie Leigh Darren Chantry (5)
Send CE Primary School, Send

Benjamin's First Riddle

What could it be?
Follow the clues and see.

It looks like **a big, long tail**.
It sounds like *hiss, hiss*.
It smells like **a log pile house**.
It feels **sticky and bumpy**.
It tastes **disgusting**.

Have you guessed what it could be?
Look below and you will see,
It is...

Answer: A rattlesnake.

Benjamin Warne (5)
Send CE Primary School, Send

Olivia's First Riddle

What could it be?
Follow the clues and see.

It looks like **blue water**.
It sounds like *splash, splash*.
It smells like **salt and seaweed**.
It feels like **water, it's wet and warm**.
It tastes like **salt**.

Have you guessed what it could be?
Look below and you will see,
It is...

Answer: *The sea.*

Olivia Lunnon (4)
Send CE Primary School, Send

Joshua's First Riddle

What could it be?
Follow the clues and see.

It looks like **the dark**.
It sounds like **when the wind howls**.
It smells like **my teddy bear**.
It feels like **soft air**.
It tastes like **a yummy dinner with sausages**.

Have you guessed what it could be?
Look below and you will see,
It is...

Answer: *Night-time.*

Joshua Patrick Lunt (5)
Send CE Primary School, Send

Florence's First Riddle

What could it be?
Follow the clues and see.

It looks like **two white balls**.
It sounds like *pat, pat, pat*.
It smells like **Christmas**.
It feels **soft and cold**.
It tastes like **ice cream**.

Have you guessed what it could be?
Look below and you will see,
It is...

Answer: A snowman.

Florence Booth (5)
Send CE Primary School, Send

Ada's First Riddle

What could it be?
Follow the clues and see.

It looks like **a round strawberry cake with candles**.
It sounds **crunchy**.
It smells like **strawberries**.
It feels **soft**.
It tastes like **strawberries and cream**.

Have you guessed what it could be?
Look below and you will see,
It is...

Answer: A cake.

Ada Reuben (4)
Send CE Primary School, Send

Mali's First Riddle

What could it be?
Follow the clues and see.

It looks **green and shiny**.
It sounds like **the breeze**.
It smells like **rosemary**.
It feels **sharp and spiky**.
It tastes like **turkey and mince pies**.

Have you guessed what it could be?
Look below and you will see,
It is...

Answer: A Christmas tree.

Mali Reuben (4)
Send CE Primary School, Send

Eve's First Riddle

What could it be?
Follow the clues and see.

It looks like **a frosty stick**.
It sounds like *drip, drip*.
It smells like **water**.
It feels **cold and slippery**.
It tastes like **cold water**.

Have you guessed what it could be?
Look below and you will see,
It is...

Answer: *An icicle.*

Eve Ellis (5)
Send CE Primary School, Send

Teddy's First Riddle

What could it be?
Follow the clues and see.

It looks like **a big, scary thing**.
It sounds like **a loud roar**.
It smells like **mud**.
It feels like **loads of lumps and spikes**.
It tastes like **meat**.

Have you guessed what it could be?
Look below and you will see,
It is...

Answer: A T-rex.

Teddy Blackwell (5)
Send CE Primary School, Send

Sophia's First Riddle

What could it be?
Follow the clues and see.

It looks **runny and bubbly**.
It sounds like *squelch, squelch*.
It smells like **flowers**.
It feels **smooth and slippery**.
It tastes like **sweets**.

Have you guessed what it could be?
Look below and you will see,
It is...

Answer: Soap.

Sophia Jessica Penny (5)
Send CE Primary School, Send

Rosie's First Riddle

What could it be?
Follow the clues and see.

It looks like **a fluffy animal**.
It sounds like *sniff, sniff*.
It smells like **grass**.
It feels like **a cuddly toy**.
You wouldn't taste it!

Have you guessed what it could be?
Look below and you will see,
It is...

Answer: A rabbit.

Rosie Walles (5)
Send CE Primary School, Send

Isla's First Riddle

What could it be?
Follow the clues and see.

It looks like **a small, round, orange fruit**.
It makes **no noise**.
It smells like **grapefruit**.
It feels **smooth**.
It tastes like **juicy fruit**.

Have you guessed what it could be?
Look below and you will see,
It is...

Answer: An orange.

Isla Wilson (5)
Send CE Primary School, Send

Alana's First Riddle

What could it be?
Follow the clues and see.

It looks like **spiky feathers**.
It sounds like **squeaky**.
It smells like **chicken**.
It feels like **needles**.
It tastes like **rabbit**.

Have you guessed what it could be?
Look below and you will see,
It is...

Answer: A hedgehog.

Alana Jean Kelly (5)
Send CE Primary School, Send

Jackson's First Riddle

What could it be?
Follow the clues and see.

It looks like **a wiggly line**.
It sounds like **sss**.
It smells like **slime**.
It feels **flat and thin**.
It tastes like **bones**.

Have you guessed what it could be?
Look below and you will see,
It is...

Answer: A snake.

Jackson James Adams (5)
Send CE Primary School, Send

Phoebe's First Riddle

What could it be?
Follow the clues and see.

It looks like **darkness**.
It sounds like **whistling**.
It smells like **a cuddly teddy bear**.
It feels **soft**.
It tastes like **honey**.

Have you guessed what it could be?
Look below and you will see,
It is...

Answer: *The wind*.

Phoebe Gayle Maritz (5)
Send CE Primary School, Send

Alexander's First Riddle

What could it be?
Follow the clues and see.

It looks **small and white**.
It sounds like **angels**.
It smells like **water**.
It feels **soft and cold**.
It tastes like **snow**.

Have you guessed what it could be?
Look below and you will see,
It is...

Answer: A snowflake.

Alexander Herwig (4)
Send CE Primary School, Send

Gracie's First Riddle

What could it be?
Follow the clues and see.

It looks like **an orange circle**.
It sounds **squeaky**.
It smells **sweet and nice**.
It feels **smooth**.
It tastes **good**.

Have you guessed what it could be?
Look below and you will see,
It is...

Answer: An orange.

Gracie Del La Rue (4)
Send CE Primary School, Send

Isla's First Riddle

What could it be?
Follow the clues and see.

It looks **big and scary**.
It sounds like **a roar**.
It smells like **smoke**.
It feels **big and rough**.
It tastes **yucky**.

Have you guessed what it could be?
Look below and you will see,
It is...

Answer: A dragon.

Isla D'Auria (4)
Send CE Primary School, Send

Theo's First Riddle

This is my riddle about a fantastic person. Who could it be? Follow the clues to see!

This person has **grey** hair,
A **crown** is what they like to wear.
They like to watch **soldiers** on TV.
They like **lobster thermidor** to eat,
And sometimes **muffins** for a treat.
A **hat** is their favourite thing.
A **prince** is their best friend,
And now this riddle is at the end.

Have you guessed who it could be?
Look below and you will see, it is…

Answer: A queen.

Theo Gibbard (4)
Shrewsbury House Pre-Preparatory School, Esher

Taran's First Riddle

This is my riddle about an amazing animal.
What could it be?
Follow the clues to see!

This animal has **scales** on its body,
And its colour is **green**.
This animal has **two** feet,
It likes **meat** to eat.
All over the Earth is where it lives,
Its favourite thing to do is **hunt**.
This animal has **zero** ears,
It makes **roaring** sounds for you to hear.

Are you an animal whiz?
Have you guessed what it is?
It is...

Answer: A dinosaur.

Taran Singh Tulsi (5)
Shrewsbury House Pre-Preparatory School, Esher

Zakaria's First Riddle

This is my riddle about an amazing animal.
What could it be?
Follow the clues to see!

This animal has **wings** on its body,
And its colour is **black**.
This animal has **two** feet,
It likes **fish** to eat.
In a jungle is where it lives,
Its favourite thing to do is **fly**.
This animal has **zero** ears.

Are you an animal whiz?
Have you guessed what it is?
It is...

Answer: A pterodactyl.

Zakaria Rafiq (4)
Shrewsbury House Pre-Preparatory School, Esher

Harley's First Riddle

This is my riddle about an amazing animal.
What could it be?
Follow the clues to see!

This animal has **spots** on its body,
And its colour is **white**.
This animal has **four** feet,
It likes **food** to eat.
In a cage is where it lives,
Its favourite thing to do is **lick**.
This animal has **two** ears.

Are you an animal whiz?
Have you guessed what it is?
It is...

Answer: A dog.

Harley Joseph Sykes (4)
Shrewsbury House Pre-Preparatory School, Esher

Ted's First Riddle

This is my super first riddle.
What could it be?
Follow the clues to see!

Scotland is where you'll find it,
It's made out of **material**.
It is used for **your country**,
Its colour is **white and blue**.
It is a **rectangle** shape,
It has **stripes**.

Have you guessed what it could be?
Look below and you will see,
It is....

Answer: The Scottish flag.

Ted William Kennedy (5)
Shrewsbury House Pre-Preparatory School, Esher

Oliver's First Riddle

What could it be?
Follow the clues and see.

It looks like **windows**.
It sounds like *rrr*.
It smells like **oil**.
It feels like **metal**.
It tastes like **nothing**.

Have you guessed what it could be?
Look below and you will see,
It is...

Answer: A car.

Oliver McIlroy (4)
Shrewsbury House Pre-Preparatory School, Esher

Charlie's First Riddle

What could it be?
Follow the clues and see.

It looks **black and white**.
It sounds like *bang*.
It smells like **plastic**.
It feels **soft**.
It tastes like **nothing**.

Have you guessed what it could be?
Look below and you will see,
It is...

Answer: A football.

Charlie Hebburn (4)
Shrewsbury House Pre-Preparatory School, Esher

George's First Riddle

What could it be?
Follow the clues and see.

It has **a roof**.
It sounds like *splash*.
It smells **smelly**.
It feels **strong**.
It tastes like **oil**.

Have you guessed what it could be?
Look below and you will see,
It is...

Answer: A bridge.

George Olivier (4)
Shrewsbury House Pre-Preparatory School, Esher

Senan's First Riddle

What could it be?
Follow the clues and see.

It looks like **a tomato**.
It sounds like **a bang**.
It smells like **smoke**.
It feels **hard**.
It tastes like **nothing**.

Have you guessed what it could be?
Look below and you will see,
It is...

Answer: A bomb.

Senan Lousse (4)
Shrewsbury House Pre-Preparatory School, Esher

Benjamin's First Riddle

What could it be?
Follow the clues and see.

It looks **brown.**
It sounds like *shh.*
It smells like **wood.**
It feels **hard.**
It tastes **yucky.**

Have you guessed what it could be?
Look below and you will see,
It is...

Answer: A boat.

Benjamin Higginson (4)
Shrewsbury House Pre-Preparatory School, Esher

Isaac's First Riddle

What could it be?
Follow the clues and see.

It looks **white**.
It sounds like **neigh**.
It smells like **dust**.

Have you guessed what it could be?
Look below and you will see,
It is…

Answer: *A horse.*

Isaac Boamah (4)
Shrewsbury House Pre-Preparatory School, Esher

Ibrahim's First Riddle

Who could it be?
Follow the clues and see.

He looks like **a bat**.
He sounds **smart**.
He feels **hard**.

Have you guessed who it could be?
Look below and you will see,
He is...

Answer: Batman.

Ibrahim Rafiq (4)
Shrewsbury House Pre-Preparatory School, Esher

YOUNG WRITERS INFORMATION

We hope you have enjoyed reading this book – and that you will continue to in the coming years.

If you're a young writer who enjoys reading and creative writing, or the parent of an enthusiastic poet or story writer, do visit our website **www.youngwriters.co.uk**. Here you will find free competitions, workshops and games, as well as recommended reads, a poetry glossary and our blog. There's lots to keep budding writers motivated to write!

If you would like to order further copies of this book, or any of our other titles, then please give us a call or order via your online account.

Young Writers
Remus House
Coltsfoot Drive
Peterborough
PE2 9BF
(01733) 890066
info@youngwriters.co.uk

Join in the conversation!
Tips, news, giveaways and much more!

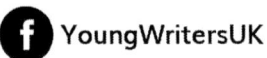 YoungWritersUK    @YoungWritersCW